You may not suspect I am sporting upcycled toilet paper roll legs at first glance. But that's one of the joys of this medium! You can re-use all sort of things to create your armatures.

Hey y'all! I'm Marti and have taught Paper Mache to beginners and art pros alike. This is a super accessible art medium that can level up your creative skills and help you become an accomplished Sculptor quickly! Ready? Let's GO!

♥ have fun!
share your projects
with #myhappyartpapermache

Hello!

I'm marti and I teach paper mâché workshops in México.

It is an ancient art medium that is inherently satisfying and easy to access for people at any level of artistic skill.

I'm looking at **YOU:**
- beginners
- 2-d artists
- hobbyists
- kiddos
- The Dali Llama (Hello Dali!)

Paper maché is one of those super adaptible art mediums that's easy to learn and offers a multitude of challenges to master.

You can do it a lot of ways.

I will show you 3 recipes with 3 fundamental armature builds.

You can use this info to make just about anything you dream up.

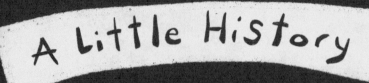

Some time during the Han Dynasty (~200 BCE) in china they invented paper, and shortly after that - paper mâché!

Of course they called it:

纸浆
"Zhǐjiāng"

or something appropriate to the lingo of the creators.

They used this new substance to create helmets and armor. Artisans honed the craft in ways that inspired mimicry across the globe.

As tradesmen traversed the oceans the skill to make durable, ornate objects out of materials increasingly easy to acquire. Persia, Kashmir (india), Europe and most especially 1700's Spain! Before you could say:

"Moctezuma's Revenge" it was imported to México where it enjoys everyday popularity to this day!

Cool! Paper mache body armor!

Early Uses of PAPER MACHÉ

Starting in 1725 in Europe, gilded p.m. began to appear as a low cost alternative to gold leafed wood carvings.

The average Joe, Jose or Josephina couldn't tell the difference. And the Saints didn't seem to mind.

Am I wood, plaster or paper maché? Doesn't matter with this 24K gold finish.

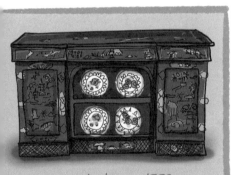

Amazingly, starting in 1772 a clever dude in England, Henry Clay, patented a paper lamination technique. You'd glue tons of BIG sheets of paper together into panels that acted a lot like plywood does these days.
They made all kinds of fancy home furnishings. They'd embellish these in an Asian style - something they'd call "Japanning". I know. I know.

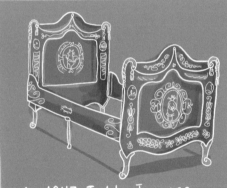

In 1847 Teddy Jennens came up with a process for steaming these laminated sheets and pressing them into moulds to dry and be assembled into even more kinds of goods.
who knew!

Paper mâché was an inexpensive and therefor popular medium for making doll heads. We're looking at the mid 1800's. First they were individually sculpted and later moulds were used to make multiples.

They were all hand painted. I don't think they were trying to make the scariest toys on earth but there sure are some rather nightmarish survivors, poor dears.

Paper Maché TOYS 1900's

Paper mâché didn't stop at creepy doll heads. Moulds were made in all kinds of adorable shapes.

We think we moderns created silly kitty memes but nope.
Our great, great grannies knew the joy of cute cats at a very young age.

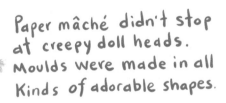

Although the craft is slowly being overtaken by manufactured plastics you can still find plenty of cartonería folk art pieces in the markets - especially during Key events on the Mexican calendar.

Sometimes you'll see old style toys in places like tourist and collector's stores.

But for sure you can find piñatas in every town.

Traditional or inspired by pop culture.

In December you'll see the pointy cone piñatas Kids smack open every night 12/16 - 12/24.

On Holy Saturday (Easter eve) all across Mexico, the faithful blow up all manner of cartoneria Judas figures. And this includes any current traitor figures. Politicians are always well represented.

Masks

show up any time there is a parade. And in San Miguel de Allende, where I live, masks are a HUGE part of the Dia de Los Locos. On this Saturday in June farmers seek to entertain the spirits of the coming rainy season.

Skeletons and skulls are a proud part of home and cemetary ofrendas (altars) all throughout the Dia de Los Muertos (Day of the dead) festivities in November.

Mojigangas
are giant wearable
puppets that dance
their way through fiestas
and parades.
Their heads are painted
cartoneria atop bamboo
structures you set on
your shoulders.
Lightweight clothes
drape over the frame
to hide the person
within.
You've got a peephole
so you don't kill
yourself or trample
chihuahuas as you
twirl all over

Hermes Arroyo and his family
are locally famous in Guanajuato state for
creating the mojigangas
that festoon the jardin
in San Miguel.
Not only that, Sr. Arroyo
also continues the art
of making religious
iconography for
churches.   He made
a life size creche for a
special display a the vatican.
Holy cows and everything!

Pedro Linares López

Was born in 1906 to a family whose business was cartoneria.
Young Pedro learned the trade in the traditional way.
But then when he was 30 years old, he slipped into a coma.

He later reported seeing all manner of colorful animals shouting the word "Alebrije! Alebrije!"

When he awoke, he began using the familiar materials of the family business to create the fantastic beings who had visited him in his visions.

Pedro's inspirited alebrije sculptures were unlike anything anyone had seen before, especially in paper.
They soon caught the eyes of México's first couple of art - Diego Rivera and Frida Kahlo. They fell in love with these dream spirits.

Alebrijes And Oaxaca

Sí! Pedro Linares López lived in Mexico City for sure, but his family is from Arrazola in Oaxaca. When he went to visit he brought some of his sculptures with him. The folks went gaga with the whole idea! But paper wasn't as easy to come by as wood in this rural region so artisans began combing the area for sticks that looked like they may already have a spirit inside just waiting to be revealed with some work and lots of paint.

Now you know that paper mâché or cartonería has a long and rich history all over the globe.

Because I'm living in México, I have a particular affinity for how it continues to be practised here. I love how many special days include hand made cartonería art objects. Holy Saturday (Judases), birthdays (piñatas) and weddings (mojigangas) to name a few.

Mexicans embrace the Grace of the unseen. But they also go to some trouble to make these joys visible.

Alebrijes, sacred icons and party elements all hold special sway here. This is a humble art form that is elevated to meaningful consequence by its specialists.

I especially appreciate how they infuse a piece with the spirit of the one being depicted - whether a corrupt political figure, blushing bride, or magical animal spirit.

I keep this in mind when I am creating my own cartoneria sculptures.

I invite you to consider spending time learning some fundamentals and then diving right in to create a piece that is meaningful to you.

This is an art form that reflects your intensions and holds space for **your dreams.**

The Main Steps

1. Decide what you want to make and sketch it. Several views is helpful.
2. Figure out how you'll construct your armature and build it!
3. Reinforce it so none of the elements are loose or floppy.
4. Make adhesive, tear paper strips and apply first layer to your armature.
5. Let dry. Prop up any droopy areas as necessary so it dries into the shape you intended.
6. Add another layer. Let dry.
7. Add paper pulp frosting and paper clay if desired. Let dry.
8. Sand out any undesired rough areas, fill in any gaps.
9. Paint base coat. Let dry.
10. Paint top layers and details.
11. Optional: Seal with Urethane
12. Add any final embellishments.

Details coming...

What you need to know to create various volumes and forms to make armatures for your paper mâché sculptures.

Armature Materials

- Newspaper or craft paper
- Cardboard
- Wire (various thicknesses)
- Masking tape

Tools

- Wire cutters
- Scissors
- Pliers

I like to encourage newbies to start with 3 fundamental armature forms.

1. mask
2. vessel
3. figure

Learning each of these will give you some experience with the mechanics and engineering of working with this medium.

you can then use these skills to create just about anything you feel like dreaming up!

The armature for your paper mâché piece has to be strong enough to hold the weight of your initial layers of adhesive soaked paper strips for as long as it takes to fully dry. Here in Mexico's central highlands during the dry season that can be as quick as 4-6 hours. In places where it's more humid it may take a couple days.

This isn't much of an issue for flat pieces like masks but for more dimensional forms, like this figure, we gotta make a sturdy armature.

From the easiest to more challenging.

You'll need:

sketch materials
Cardboard
Scissors
news or craftpaper
masking tape
Wire (12-14 guage is good)

#1. A Mask

to hang on a wall.
You can make wearable masks as
your skills grow.

make a sketch

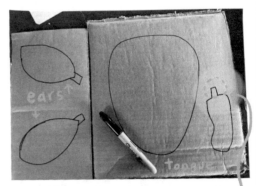

Draw the main shapes onto
cardboard.
Add a tab for taping...

Position the pieces.
Note the tabs on the ears and tongue.

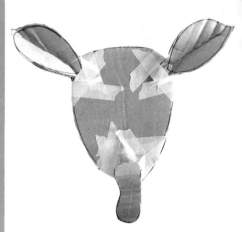

Add dimension by slicing part way and bending.
Tape into position.

Build up volume with crumpled paper and tape away, kiddo.

This is the stage where it's the best time to create the most bulk of your sculpture.

You can add details as you go like these teeth and chops.

Keep on adding bulk and taping firmly.

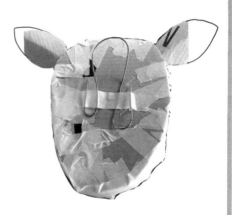

Bend your wire to form a hanger and tape well to the back.

Tape that wire on real well. Criss cross your tape. Leave the hanger part untaped.

You're done when you have the volumes you want and everything feels nice and sturdy.

Pro Tip: You can use ANY non-breakable bowl, cup, box or dish as an armature. Craft stores often sell ready-made styrofoam forms.

But this a How-to book, so lets start from scratch.

You'll need:
- sketch materials
- cardboard
- scissors
- news or craft paper
- masking tape

2. A Bowl

To store or display non-liquid things.

You can make this fancy, strange, whimsical, large or small.

Make it yours!

Here's how....

the bottom will be cardboard

make a simple drawing of your bowl. I'm going a little silly.

↑ The Bottom

sketch the main shapes onto cardboard and cut out.

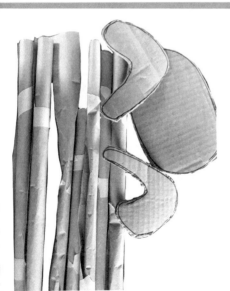

Roll up a bunch of tubes using newspaper or brown craft paper.

Start taping a tube onto your bowl's cardboard base. Keep going around and up.

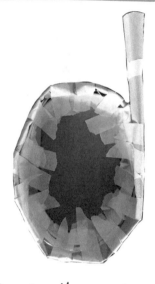

Basically you're taping a paper coil 'round and 'round.

It's not very pretty or sturdy at this point.

As you proceed you can go as high as you like. And you can squeeze and tape more firmly once you're done with the first pass.

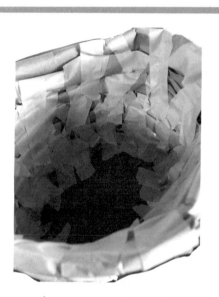

Looking inside. A bit of a mess - but let's keep going!

Here's the outside. It's about as tall as I want to go. So next I'm going to squeeze and tape to make it firm.

A little peek at the bottom at this point.

You can see now that I've started to smoosh the sides and tape them firmly. Up and down and sideways, too.

Time to add the detail forms. In this case, a couple of ears.

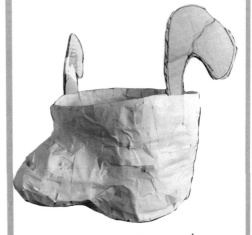

Finally, I finish my vessel armature by attaching paper balls to make a muzzle.

Now you've got a good idea of how to start a successful armature using some simple materials.

Let's level it up by creating a standing figure. Or, if you like, design this piece to be suspended.

You'll need:

- sketch materials
- news or craft paper
- Wire, 12-14 guage is good
- needlenose pliers
- masking tape

Make your sketch. Draw it from a couple angles to work out the main volumes if this is among your first figures.

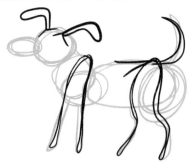

The grey lines show how you might create the main geometries out of taped paper crumples.

The black depicts how you might add the wire for legs, tail and ears.

I've started with the main body. Paper and tape.

More paper and tape! Also I bent some wire for the tail.

← It's taped to the rump like this.

A view of the tail wire taped along the back. This adds stabilty.

It's smart to sort of over build your structure like this.

It will help prevent cracks later.

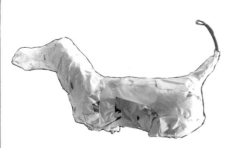

Continue adding paper volume to the figure. Depending on the pose and level of realism you're after you may build up familiar or fanciful muscle shapes.

Time to add the legs. I go up and over the back to maximize stability.

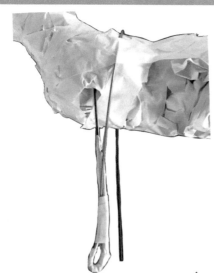

I'll reinforce the single wire by taping on some reinforcing lengths.

I'll do this for all the legs. When I bend the wire at the ends using some needlenose pliers I make sure to adjust the legs so my piece will stand square on all fours. Do that now. It's so much harder later.

As your figure begins to reveal itself, it becomes more intuitive where you need to adjust, add bulk and tweak. It starts helping you build itself!

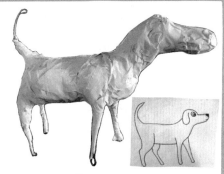

Keep referring back to your original sketches to ensure you maintain a fairly high fidelity to your original plan. **OR** let your construction process participate in the design result.

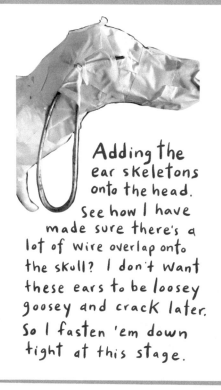

Adding the ear skeletons onto the head. See how I have made sure there's a lot of wire overlap onto the skull? I don't want these ears to be loosey goosey and crack later. So I fasten 'em down tight at this stage.

This dude's armature is just about complete...

Let's make sure our armatures are ready for the first layer of adhesive and paper strips, ok?

How to check:

- **Does it feel firm to the touch?**
  No? Tape loose areas by pressing one end of each length of tape and stretch and pull as you smooth it down.

- **Any loosey-goosey appendiges?**
  Firm any wiggly bits with tape. Do it now – or these areas most likely will crack later.

- **Have you got most of the overall volume you want?**
  The adhesive and frosting layers will add about 1/4 -1/3" or 1/2 -1 cm

- **Are all your bits where you want them?**
  No? Hork 'em into position and tape in place. This gets hard to correct later.

A collection of sample armatures

This one began with an empty water bottle and sticks.

a   b

This flying piggie is wired tightly to a weighty rock. He has cardboard wings.

I used tin foil for the bulk of this pupper.

Here's the armature for a serving tray

This grazing horse has random sticks for legs.

This one will hang on the wall.

(It's inspired by a Frida Kahlo painting)

I paid very close attention to where that one foot attaches to the rock on the cardboard base. lots of extra wire goes around the stone and up the leg and body.

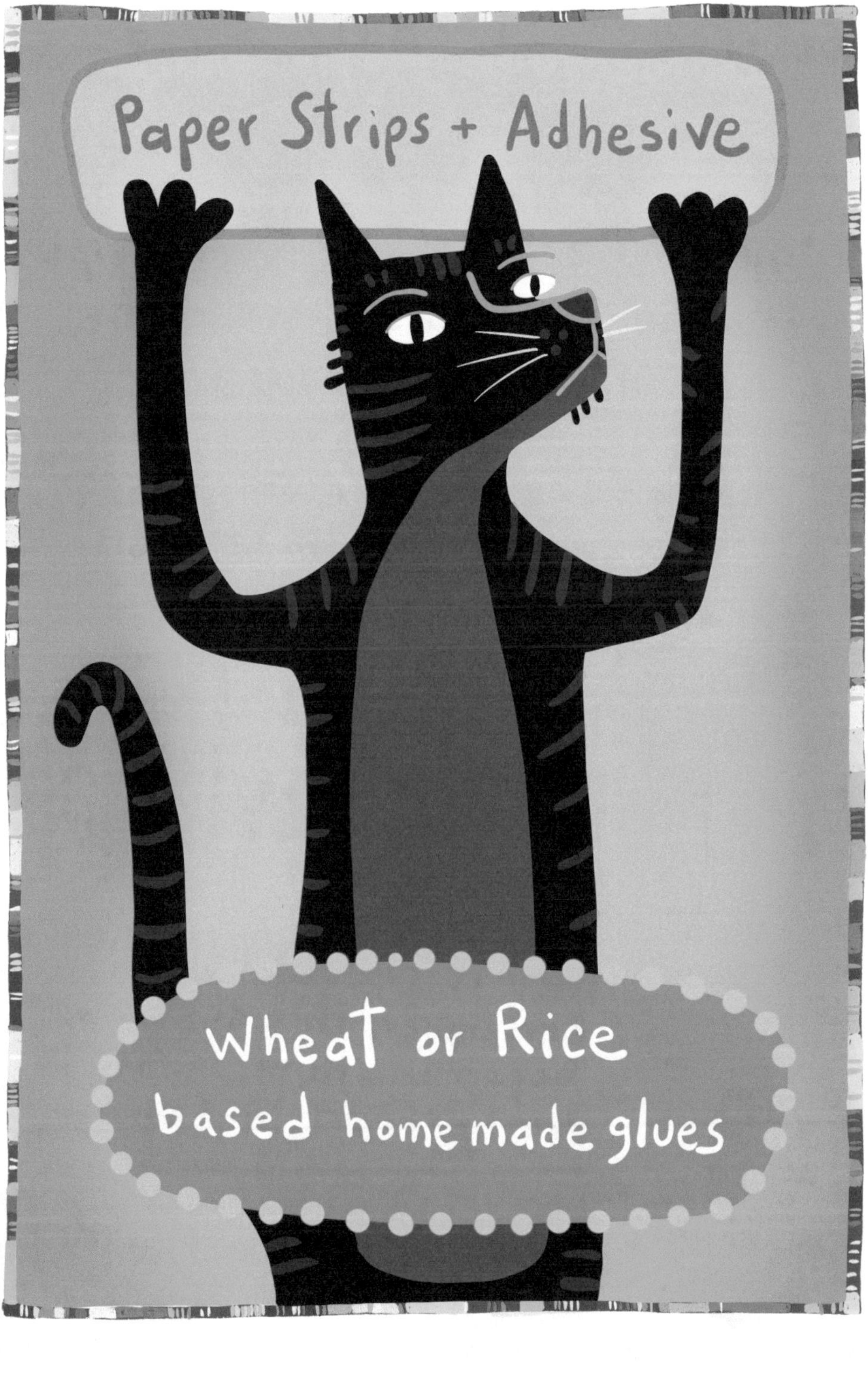
Paper Strips + Adhesive
Wheat or Rice based home made glues

Homemade Adhesives

Your armature is ready, let's mix up a glue to attach paper strips that will dry and harden the piece into a unified whole.

Through the years 2 main types of base ingredients have been used.

Wheat is great because it contains glutin. GLUtin, get it? Glutin makes a wonderful adhesive.

But, so does **Rice**.

Rice is super old school. Remember, this art form began in China, so rice is likely the original choice.

I use the wheat recipe mostly because it cooks up fast.

Wheat Adhesive Recipe

You'll need:

- Burner
- Pan
- whisk
- Big spoon
- measuring cup

Ingredients:

- 1 cup white wheat flour
- 1/4 cup corn starch
- 2T vinegar
- 1T PVA glue like Elmer's
- 2 cups water

Tips

- don't use whole wheat flour - not as sticky.
- don't use glutin-free flour. You want the glue.
- The vinegar will prevent mold growing if it takes too long to dry or gets too humid later.
- The PVA glue is optional
  OR
  can be watered down and used instead of the wheat adhesive.
- The vinegar will help lengthen the life of any leftover adhesive you store in the fridge BUT the gluten will weaken. Try not to mix more than you will use in 24 hours, or so.

Directions:

- whisk all the ingredients in the pan over medium heat.
- It will thicken. Keep whisking briskly so you don't get lumps.
- If it's too runny, cook down. If it's too thick add water 1/4 cup at a time.
- You want it to be like a thick gravy. When it is - it's ready!

Rice Adhesive Recipe

You'll need:

- Burner
- Pan
- Wooden spoon
- measuring cup

Ingredients:

- 1 cup basmati or sushi rice
- 3-4 cups water

- Unlike the wheat glue this adhesive does not lose stickiness when stored.
- when soaked with water this glue will release.
- This glue is completely archival - it's acid-free.

Directions:

Boil the rice and then turn the heat down and simmer for 45 minutes. stir occasionally.

Cook until the stuff looks like porridge. If it's still too granular just add some more water and keep simmering.

When the rice finally starts to break down, remove from heat. let cool.

Plop into a blender and blend on high.

Adjust the thickness by adding a bit of water. You want a consistency akin to gravy.

Cooking the rice

when it soaks up the first water...

Add more!
Keep simmering.

Stir occasionally.

Cook until the rice really softens.

Remove from heat and blend smooth.

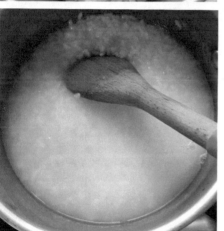

Paper & Adhesive

wheat or rice

newsprint
Craft paper

Tear (don't cut, you want the rough edges) the paper into pieces about 1.5" x 3".

You'll discover that newspaper tears more easily in one direction. You can control the width of your strips tearing along the grain.

You can use almost any non-glossy paper. It just needs to be able to absorb your adhesive.

You'll probably use 3-4 large sheets of craft paper or half of a typical newspaper section per sculpture about the sizes I'm making for the demos in this book. All are about 10" x 10" or a little less.

Serve yourself about a cup of adhesive into a shallow dish.

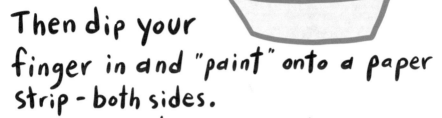

Then dip your finger in and "paint" onto a paper strip - both sides.
Smooth onto the armature.
Overlap the next one a bit.

  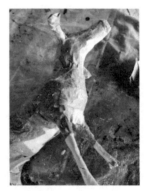

Making progress on the demos.
First layer. I'll let dry and do a second layer for each.

Here's what the demos look like with 2 full layers of adhesive strips applied.

When dry you can stop right here. Maybe sand off any rough areas and begin Painting.

I'm going to paper-frost these pieces next.

Paper Pulp
Frosting & Clay

Two techniques that can add strengh, texture and details to your pieces.

Uses some of the magical properties of cheap toilet paper.

Paper Pulp Frosting Recipe

This concoction can elevate your paper mache pieces from the world of crafts into the realm of fine art. Try it at least once and decide for yourself.

You'll need:

- 1 cup of wheat or rice adhesive
- 1 cup of gypsum based joint compound dry or wet - either works!
  You'll just need less water if you use wet.
- 1 roll of plain, unscented, non-moisturizer toilet paper.
- 1 T PVA (Elmer's white or similar)
- Extra wheat flour
- Water as necessary

- Mixing bowl
- Hand mixer

Get "joint compound" wherever they carry drywall/sheetrock supplies

1. place roll of t.p. in bowl. Add a couple of inches of water.
The t.p. will drink it up! Flip the roll for maximum absorption. Take the cardboard tube out. Should lift right out.
pour off any excess water.

2. Reach in and tear into chunks. They'll be good and soggy.

3. Take your hand mixer and mix up the chunks.
They'll turn out something like this pulpy! ⟶
You can also run through a blender or food processor.

4. With a spoon or your hands mix in the other ingredients. Mix up until it looks like frosting.

Here's what the paper pulp frosting looks like when it's ready.

I'm going to use those brushes and my fingers to apply to the sculptures I've got ready.

flimsy plastic paddles work super great!

I'm starting with applying by hand to the 3 sample sculptures I've got going.

This is a glop and smooth activity.

Fingers are a very handy tool. Literally, right? You can gently push the frosting into tricky locations.

This medium will hold its form as you apply it and reposition your piece for full coverage.

And you can apply on one side, let dry, and finish another day.

Store any leftover paper pulp frosting up to a week in the fridge.

I use a brush at times to smooth the frosting.

You can smooth more when dry by sanding.

Here are the 3 sculptures fully frosted, but before any sanding.

I can file or sand off these "burrs".

They took about 36 hours to dry completely. Dry-time is related to the amount of humidity in the air.

Paper Clay

I like to add details to my pieces using a paper clay I make using leftover (or make more) paper frosting.

Just add more white wheat flour to some paper frosting. How much? Kind of depends on how much you're making.

Mix it in until it resembles bread dough. Knead it smooth with a dusting of flour.

You can use the paper clay pretty much like you would plasticene or similar stuff.
I glue it in place using extra rice or wheat adhesive.
I paint it on with a brush.

This is great for adding dimension and decorations you can later paint.

I use a variety of sandpaper grit sizes.
From coarse (40-60)
to medium (80)
to fine (100-120)
Fold or roll pieces to reach the odd area.
Round files work well, too.

Filling in little holes

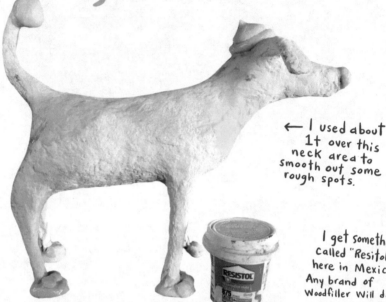

← I used about 1t over this neck area to smooth out some rough spots.

I get something called "Resitol" here in Mexico. Any brand of Woodfiller will do.

Woodfiller works great! Plus you can paint on it before it dries, if you're impatient like I can be. :)

Perfect for dinky holes like this.

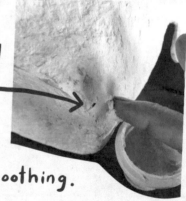

Smoosh in with your finger. Then taper it away by pressing and smoothing.

The 3 sample pieces are ready for paint!

- ☑ Armatured
- ☑ paper mached
- ☑ frosted
- ☑ detailed
- ☑ filled
- ☑ Sanded

There are a variety of media you can use to finish a paper mache piece.

Pretty much anything you can envision is worth trying!

- collage (tissue paper, printed paper, hand painted paper, fabric, etc.)
- Glued found objects, yarn, string, flowers, glitter, etc.)
- Dripped wax, melted crayons, etc.
- or my favorite: PAINT!

Water color · Gouach · Acrylic

Flat · Glossy · Metallic Glitter!

Since I've got 3 samples prepped I'm going to demo 3 types of paint techniques.

If you already have paint you like to use - I can pretty much guarantee it can work to paint your paper mache pieces. Experiment!

I like to go with:

1. Bright acrylic base coat with acrylic top layers.

2. Black acrylic base coat with regular and metallic acrylic top layers.
This really can highlight the TEXTURE of your sculpture.

3. White acrylic base coat with gouache and water color top layers
Excellent for layering hues.

Here's samples of each of these :

1
Bright base coat Acrylic top coats

3
White base coat Gouache and Water color top coats

2
Black base coat, multi-color and metallic top coats

Time to get to the three samples!

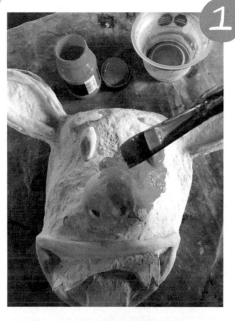

1

Bright Acrylic undercoat

Tip: Dip your brush in Water to help spread the paint

Use a brush you don't mind Smooshing into nooks + crannies.

Paint the back, too!

Be sure to get paint into these low areas.

2 Black acrylic undercoat.
Tip: Spray the piece with water to help spread the paint.

Slap the paint on and smoosh into crevices.

Don't forget the inside...
... and bottom.

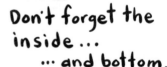

3 White or very light acrylic Base coat.

Using a small amount of color helps you differeniate from the sculpture's paper frosting layer.

You can see the yellow wood filler and the white of the dried paper mulche frosting. I used a lightly tinted base coat

Top Bottom Sides full coverage!

I'm over painting my tinted first coat because I want the transparency of the coming watercolor paint to play off a bright white surface.

This piece already has 2 layers of acrylic paint.

The acrylic paint helps make the sculpture water-proof.

Once the bright
base coat
is fully
dry, I go
back in and
begin layering the upper
layers of acrylic paint.

In low textured areas my brush
may bounce off leaving a peek
of the undercoat.
This adds depth to the look of
the piece in its final state.

Because I used something other
than white, it looks more
intentional.

You can experiment all you
like! Mix it up. Have fun.

In the spots you can see the original hot pink.

Also in the ear and mouth inners.

Meanwhile I'm also layering up greens and blues.

Here's a bit of a closer look.

I want my paint mottled rather than "flat" monochromes.

I begin what will become the metallic piece with regular acrylics.

I'm choosing colors I know will look good with the final paint layers.

I'm definitely preserving the texture of the piece by using a very light touch with my brush.

Don't forget the inside and bottom.

Ready for the
next layer of
paint!

See how the base
coat black still
peeks through
in places?

Time to brush
on the shiny
metallic
paints!
Again I'm
using a very
light touch
with that
flat brush.

This vessel is about ready for the final paint touches.

If I decided I'd lost too much of the texture of the black undercoat, I could daub on some more black and over paint when dry. This is a very forgiving medium.

On top of the nice white acrylic paint base coats I'm going to use gouache and water colors.

I can get away with this sort of sacrilige better if I use a white gesso.
But, honestly, I find my gouache and pan-based

water colors work just fine and don't "bead up". If they did I'd just use more OR watered down acrylics.

As you can see, the paints are going on great!

I'm going to build on this mottling and texture.

I've painted a couple light layers at this stage.

I listen to podcasts and audiobooks as I obsessively attend to the details.

Trust me, this is a calming process. Great for turbulent news cycles.

I go back and overlay the semitransparent paints with some flourescent acrylics. But that's just me.

Here are the finished sample pieces.

I painted on some final details.

I darkened some areas with a diluted black wash.

You could seal each sculpture with varnish or polyurethane.

You can use a spray or brush on Varnish or Urethane to seal your sculpture. Oil or Water based. This Will make it more Waterproof. Make sure it's fully dry before you seal.

If you painted with gouache or water colors - you may want to fix those layers before brushing on sealant.

Dimensional Painting

ok. So not everyone wants to work on sculptures or objects.

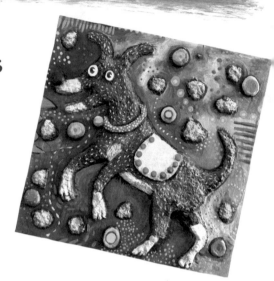

Some artists are way more interested in Painting and collage. I get it. I got you. I've been experimenting with using a combo of paper mache and paper pulp frosting on flat boards. I sketch out an idea and then build up the surface. First with the frosting. Then I sort of glue down potential edges with slurry soaked mini strips of Kraft paper.

Tips

- use board - not canvas - you need the stability to minimize cracking potential.

- rough up the surface with sandpaper.

- Apply your paper frosting and paper clay.

- "tape" any edges with adhesive and paper strips.

- let dry fully

- prime and paint! Any paint medium will work

inspirations

students' pieces

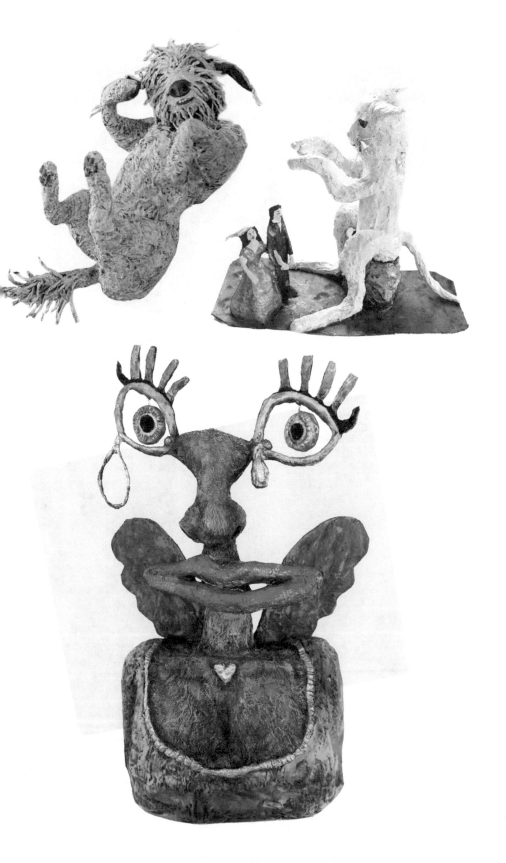

a few more finished pieces...

home decor

MasK

TiPS

CLEAN UP

- put a screen strainer in your sink's drain to catch the lumps and clumps.

- Wash your hands with a dish scrubbie

- Use a bucket filled with water for your main wash up. Dump outside somewhere lumps won't matter.

TEXTURE

- skip the paper frosting and stick paper globs and twisted ribbons.

- Add sand, Kitty litter or other flotsam to your paper frosting.

Experiment!
   - leaves
   - string
   - non clumping Kitty litter
   - crumpled foil bits
   - ribbon
   - cardboard nibs
   - etc

View & Share

If you're curious, I have a free Video series that walks you through the whole process in Real time.

Videos   www.happyart.com/paper-mache

Share your pix!

On your social media add the hashtag:

#myhappyartpapermache

- TikTok
- Instagram
- X
- Facebook
- YouTube
  etc

Made in United States
Troutdale, OR
09/21/2024

23009646R00051